THE C

BY

HENRY FREEMAN

© 2016 Copyright

No part of this book may be reproduced in any form or by any electronic or mechanical means including information storage and retrieval systems, without permission in writing from the author.

Introduction

In light of the absolute brutality of ISIS who has been raping, murdering and enslaving religious minorities all over Iraq, Syria, and Lebanon, the Pope of the Catholic Church has recently called for immediate intervention. And then rather predictably immediately after Pope Francis made this appeal he was bombarded with criticism and vitriol and likened to none other than Pope Urban II, the Pope who had issued the very first Crusade 1000 years before.

In the modern lexicon, "Crusades" and "Crusader" are words often hurled at Christians in derision as if they are something to be ashamed of. But those hurling the abuse more often than not don't have the slightest idea what they are talking about. For these ill-informed individuals, the crusades were just a bunch of illiterate, drunken Europeans of the dark ages who forced their way onto Islamic territory just to cause trouble for no reason whatsoever.

This of course, couldn't be farther from the truth, and to know the real reason why Urban the II called for a Crusade in 1099 AD, you don't have to look much further than to what ISIS is doing today. Then, just like now, Islamic armies were killing, raping and enslaving innocent people all over the Mid-East in the name of Islam.

Many people like to refer to ISIS as the "so-called" Islamic state and point out that nothing they do is in any way Islamic. But the fact remains that they themselves believe they are Muslims and they are most certainly not killing in the name of Karl Marx or Joseph Smith, they are killing in the name of Islam. And whether people want to admit it or not, it is an undeniable fact that Islam was forged in the bloodshed of war.

How do you think Egypt, Syria, Libya and Iraq; countries that were all predominantly Christian at one time, all became almost completely Islamic? Do you think benevolent Muslim missionaries managed to convert the masses through a lot of good outreach programs, charitable work, preaching, praying and the handing out of religious tracts? No, sadly enough, all of these countries had been forcibly converted by the sword, to Islam; historians cannot deny this fact.

And so it was, that after almost all of North Africa and the Mid-East had fallen to the sword, Islamic leaders began to set their eyes on Europe, which seemed ripe for conversion and conquest. Except in those days the boundaries of Europe were a bit larger, because this place that we call Turkey today, was once a part of the Greek Byzantine Empire and the Eastern most boundary of Christian Europe.

As much as Turkey is struggling to gain membership in the European Union in recent years, it is still a very uncomfortable truth when they have to deal with their own past, and how it was that their nation even came into being in the first place. Because much like the sad story of the Native Americans, the Native Greeks of Anatolia were swallowed up by Islamic armies, murdered and bartered off into slavery. And as the once great city of Constantinople, the capitol of the Eastern half of the Roman Empire was renamed Istanbul; the Christian Byzantines were no more.

It was in order to prevent this coming holocaust that Pope Urban the II had called upon all the able-bodied men of Europe to selflessly leave behind everything they had ever known; their friends, family and property, in order to risk life and limb defending their besieged Christian brothers in the East. This was the whole reason for the original call for a Crusade, not to attack, but to defend those who were being attacked.

The true reason for the conflict has been greatly twisted for various reasons throughout history, but we can find the roots of some of the most prominent propaganda against the real motive of the Crusades, in a place that might surprise you; The Protestant Reformation. Because it was at this time; hundreds of years after the Crusades, that Protestant Christians breaking away from the Vatican took a severe anti-Catholic stance in everything the Church said or did.

But in 1529, even the German Monk Martin Luther recanted and saw the folly in his criticism when the Ottoman Empire rolled right through Hungary and threatened to knock down the very gates of Vienna, Austria, just a few miles from the Protestant leader's residence.

Then, just like today, there is just something about having mass murderers ringing your door bell that makes you start to change your mind. And just as Luther made a complete 360 in his stance, many of even the most strident of Anti-Western thinkers are beginning to wise up as well, as they see ISIS for the unwavering hatred and brutality they represent, bent on nothing short of decimating anyone different from them.

Pope Francis wept over the senseless violence that has murdered thousands of Christians throughout the Middle East since the rise of ISIS and has called for the world to stop an "unjust aggressor." And no matter your stance of what the facts of over 1000 years ago might represent to you, you can't blame the many suffering and very real, tortured souls of today, who are looking to the pontiff for one last crusade.

CHAPTER 1

Backing Up Byzantium

"On Tuesday May 29, 1453, the sultan took possession of our City; in this time of capture my late master and emperor, Lord Constantine, was killed. I was taken prisoner and suffered the evils of wretched slavery. Finally I was ransomed on September 1,, 1453 and departed for Mistra. My wife and children were sold to the Sultan's Mir Ahor (Master of the Horse) who had amassed a great fortune by selling many other beautiful noble ladies."

The above quote is an eyewitness testimony from a former courtier who lived through the fall of Constantinople, the capitol of the Byzantine Empire. His horrific story of devastation was exactly what the Crusades had been created to prevent. Constantinople's first official appeal for help from the Roman Catholic Church occurred in 1095 when Emperor Alexius Comnensus sent a special delegation on a mission to Piacenza, Italy to ask on his behalf for the assistance of the Pope.

It was this special envoy that led to the council of Clermont, France on November 27, 1095, in which Pope Urban the II called for the first crusade in an effort to help defend the Byzantines and prevent the Muslim advance in Europe. This was not just some random whim, it was an official call to arms of all men capable of enough to make the journey and through further commiseration with the leaders and lords of Europe a start date of August 15, 1096 was declared as the launch date of the first Crusade.

Hailing rather far from Rome, it was actually the Norwegian King Sirgud who scored the first victory of the crusades, his crack unit of troops successfully put down two substantially larger Turkish forces at Dorylaeum and Antioch. The battle of Antioch being the most important victory, since it was the ancient and revered site of many of the early missions of the Gospel, including even the "Cave Church of St. Peter".

But beyond the sacredness of the site, Antioch was of extreme strategic importance as well. Antioch was a fortress city whose walls were built by the Byzantine Emperor Justinian, hundreds of years before, at the height of the Byzantine Empire. Wresting this fortified city from the Muslims was deemed to be a strategic first foothold on route to reclaiming the Holy Land.

The Siege of Antioch lasted for over seven and a half long months and for the Crusaders waiting outside the gates of the city, conditions were miserable. But the Muslim occupiers of Antioch were not exactly ready for a standoff. Antioch, a long time holdout for the Byzantines, had only just fallen to the Muslims about ten years before, in 1085, the loss of this fortress city being one of the main grievances highlighted by the Byzantines in their pleas to the west for help.

And in that short window of ten years, the Muslim occupiers barely had the time to get a foothold for themselves, making the city the perfect staging ground for the first Crusader rescue mission. After defeating two relief armies sent to stop them, one from Syria and one from Iraq, the Crusaders finally determined that it was time to retake the city.

The best way to do this soon proved to be a subterfuge when someone on the inside of the city betrayed the Turks and let the Crusaders right in through the gate. And then after becoming the gate crashers that the Turks never wanted, a brief battle ensued, the conclusion of which left Antioch once again in Christian hands. And thanks to this first Crusade, the Byzantines, were able to reassert their control in much of Anatolia and the Muslim advance that had previously threatened their existence would be pushed back for a few more centuries.

But although the Crusaders gave much breathing space to the beleaguered Byzantines, they did not entirely keep their original bargain with Constantinople and instead of relinquishing Antioch and many other previously Byzantine lands immediately back to the Empire, they kept it for themselves and thus created the Crusader state principality of Antioch. Here the Crusaders spent a few years in recuperation and reorganization before marching further south in 1099 towards the greatest prize of all; Jerusalem.

CHAPTER 2

All Out Holy War

The group that made this pilgrimage was a much smaller force than the army that besieged Antioch, but these troops were hardened crack soldiers. The only problem with these battle-worn warriors was that like many soldiers who are overstressed and overburdened fighting wars far from their homeland, many started to develop severe psychological fatigue and states of mind that can only be described as PTSD.

And this psychological strain on the Crusaders seemed to come to a head during the bizarre episode of Peter Bartholomew's trial by fire during the siege of the Muslim town of Arqa. Peter Bartholomew was a French soldier who participated in the siege of Antioch. Bartholomew would later claim to be experiencing all manner of visions, and divine revelation, including one in which he recounts observing beings dressed in "brilliant garments" who were "fair beyond the sons of man."

Bartholomew's odd behavior began shortly after the acquisition of Antioch when he claimed to have recovered the "Holy Lance" (the Roman spear that pierced Christ). Sometimes known as the Spear of Destiny, the find of this supposed Holy Relic boosted the morale of the tired and half-starved Crusaders who remained. The Crusader authorities didn't know if the claim was true or false, but after seeing the significant boost to their soldier's enthusiasm, they remained silent on the issue.

Many of the Crusaders did indeed look at this find as a sign of God's approval and as further evidence, as they journeyed onward to Jerusalem, many of them even began to have visions as their own; making claims of seeing celestial warriors on horseback riding to their aid. Whether these were some kind of starvation/exhaustion induced hallucinations no one really knows. But whatever it was, these men who were greatly outnumbered and by all accounts should have been on their last leg, fought with such a ferocious fervor that they managed to scare the crap out of any Islamic forces that tried to stand against them.

Many took these incredible victories as a validation of Peter Bartholomew's relic of the spear but even so, others still had their doubts and desired proof. Desiring to put to rest any concern about the spear's authenticity once and for all, in April of 1099, just outside of Arqa, Bartholomew declared his desire for a literal "trial by fire". This was a strange medieval concept that you could employ in order to prove you are telling the truth by running through flames.

Other soldiers obliged his request and set up two piles of blazing wood parallel to each other, creating a narrow passage for Peter to walk through. With the fire roaring, Peter then attempted to traverse the flames holding the spear. Unfortunately for Peter whatever he thought was going to happen did not occur and he emerged from the flames severely burned and would end up dying a painful death a little over a week later.

Some alternative accounts of this story attempt to claim that Peter did in fact, emerge from the flames unscathed, protected by the spear, but was injured when the excited crowd rushed toward him to praise the miracle. Most historians believe the latter account to be false, however, and chronicled that Peter Bartholomew was most likely burned to death in the trial by fire that he himself had insisted upon.

This tragic event clearly demonstrates that even though the Crusaders were excellent fighters whose ferocity could not be matched in battle, many like Peter were starting to become mentally unglued. For many, the search for Holy Relics such as the spear began to supersede even the original mission of reclaiming Christian lands.

It has been said that the Crusades were notoriously bad for plunder with most participants going broke for the mission rather than gaining any wealth, but even though Gold wasn't to be found, items perceived to have some sort of religious power or connotation were never in short supply.

And as a result the knights of Europe found themselves scrambling all over the Mid-East to uncover supposed relics from the Christian past. The most mythic of these relics of course, was the Holy Grail, an item that would echo throughout the lore for centuries. This cup of Christ believed to have been used at the last supper was said to give eternal life to anyone who drank from it.

But on the outskirts of Jerusalem in 1099 AD, it was a challenge for the weary Crusaders to even get a drink of water let alone eternal life. As they waited outside the gates, it became increasingly hard to find a reliable water source, and for the 15,000 some fighters waiting at the gate, death by dehydration seemed like a real possibility. The only immediately available water source was about 6 miles away and the Crusaders had to risk constant attack and ambush from Muslim soldiers who would lay in wait for them, knowing the situation was grim the leadership of the Crusading force decided that it was now or never and issued the command to attack.

The remaining Crusaders then strategically placed themselves right in front of the city walls and it was here the men managed to finally quench their thirst. It was right below the south wall at the "Pool of Siloam" that they finally found untainted drinking water. The site of this water, however, almost unleashed pandemonium as the thirst-crazed c soldiers began to fight themselves over access to the pool.

One of the leaders of the Crusade, Raymond d'Aguilers, painted a grim picture when he testified that, "Those who were strong pushed and shoved their way in a deathly fashion through the pool, which was already choked with dead animals and men struggling for their lives, and reached the rocky mouth of the fountain, while those who were weaker were left behind in the filthy water. These weaker ones sprawled on the ground with gaping mouths, their parched tongues making them speechless, while they stretched out their hands to beg water from the more fortunate ones."

A very desperate scene indeed; and these men half delusional from lack of food and water hardly seemed like a successful siege force, but nevertheless, the plan to take the city continued. It was in the midst of these final chaotic plans that some of the leaders of the army risked a pilgrimage to the Mount of Olives. Where, as legend has it, they met a strange old hermit who lived in the area, and for some reason it was this wizened old man who managed to convince these European Crusaders to go ahead and launch their attack on Jerusalem the next day.

According to the Crusade leaders' own testimony, they asserted that this mysterious hermit was adamant with them that they could succeed, "if only they had enough faith." This is, like many of the accounts of what actually happened during the Crusades, an account that seems to defy logic and belief. But whatever actually happened on the Mount of Olives history does record well what happened the next day.

The Crusaders successfully overran the outer defenses of Jerusalem and according to all Arab accounts of the attack, the defenders were mostly caught off guard and deeply astonished at the ferocity and fanaticism of the Crusader onslaught. The hardened Crusaders were prepared to fight to the death and hurled themselves without any sign of fear or hesitation at the Muslim fortifications.

But this enthusiasm would soon wane and even after breaching the outer walls, the inner walls protecting the city still remained and the Crusaders realized that no matter how ferocious the warriors were, the 50 foot high inner walls of the city would require more than ferocity in order for them to breach the city. The Crusaders then looked to the nearby port of Jaffa where they had just received word that 2 Genoese Galleys and 4 British ships had just arrived on shore with fresh supplies.

These vessels came stocked with food and armaments and more importantly for the task at hand, they came equipped with the much needed hardware to build a siege engine, so the Crusaders could finally tear down the walls of Jerusalem. But before the Crusaders could utilize these fresh supplies they had to get there first, and even sending out battalions the short distance to Jaffa was a trip filled with peril. Leadership immediately dispatched a group of 50 knights and 50 infantry to collect the goods, but as soon as this group left it was decided that reinforcements should be added and so Lord Raymond Piletus and fifty of his knights were sent after them.

This turned out to be very wise thinking because on the way to the port of Jaffa, the initial Crusader force of 100 was ambushed by an Islamic force of 600, the Crusaders were surrounded and fought desperately to break through but were quickly overwhelmed and began to suffer high casualties. All seemed to be lost for these men until a dust cloud on the horizon seemed to indicate that their deliverance was at hand. With their horses running at full charge through the desert sands, the reinforcement of Lord Raymond Piletus and his knights had arrived.

Taken completely off guard by this heavy cavalry charge of armored knights, the Muslim fighters rapidly went from the offensive to the defensive and soon abandoned the fight all together, deciding to make a hasty retreat. The knights then chased after them and managed to kill 200 of them as they fled, making it an all-around disastrous defeat for the Muslim force. After the remaining knights escorted the supply line back to the gates of Jerusalem, with the help of a few Genoese engineers, the Crusaders began working on constructing a massive battering ram, siege engines and catapults to take the city.

The final battle for Jerusalem occurred on July 13, 1099; this fighting force now consisted of 12,000 regular soldiers and 1200 knights. In the first leg of the assault the battering ram was taken to the northern wall just to the east of Herod's Gate and used to bust through the barrier. The Crusaders immediately poured through this breach in a hail of stones and arrows that the defenders frantically launched at them.

Meanwhile, one of the huge siege engines was put in place right outside the wall; ready to unleash an attack. As the siege engine inched closer, the Muslim defenders started launching catapults of a flaming substance that was known as "Greek Fire," a mysterious invention of the ancient Greeks that the Muslims had acquired, which involved flinging a substance akin to modern napalm on their enemies.

Over and over again, the siege engines were set ablaze, but just as quickly the Crusaders down below put out the fire with mixtures of water and vinegar that they had on hand thanks to their Genoese supply line. After several instances of this, one of the Siege engines was destroyed, killing many Crusaders in the process. But despite the casualties, the Crusaders continued to coordinate with their remaining Siege engine until they finally managed to make contact with the wall and after even more vigorous fighting the Siege engine's bridge was lowered and the Crusaders gained a foothold into the city.

The defenders soon gave up after this and many of the Muslim fighters ran to the Al Aqsa mosque to seek refuge there. After agreeing to pay the knights a large ransom, the Muslims finally surrendered to the Crusaders and the knights then proceeded to proudly display the banner of their benefactor Count Tancred over the mosque to celebrate their victory. The Governor, who had been holed up with a small force in the tower of David, surrendered shortly after this and was allowed to peacefully leave the city; leaving Jerusalem once again in Christian hands.

CHAPTER 3

The Kingdom of Heaven

The Kingdom of Jerusalem was a Crusader Kingdom that was founded in 1099 shortly after the First Crusade. The first incarnation of this Kingdom was in the various captured cities that the Crusaders had managed to cobble together after the initially Crusading effort. The Crusaders, coming from a Medieval Feudal system, brought their system of governance with them and as some historians have quipped, they brought to the Holy Land their "Vassals and Castles".

Mostly cut off from Western Europe, this Kingdom initially had close ties with the Byzantine Empire and the Kingdom of Armenia. The territory of this Kingdom encompassed much of the modern State of Israel along with the West Bank, Lebanon and parts of Syria and Egypt. The first man to rule the Kingdom of Jerusalem was Godfrey of Bouillon on July 22, 1099; Godfrey was by all accounts a very courageous knight and hailed from the same very same order that would eventually spawn the legendary Knights Templar.

Godfrey was also a devoutly religious man and it was said that he refused to take the crown as King because he felt it wrong to wear a crown of gold in the city where Jesus Christ wore a crown of thorns. Denouncing the official title of King, Godfrey was unofficially known as simply, "Defender of the Holy Sepulcher". Godfrey would die less than a year later and leadership would then fall onto the shoulders of his brother Baldwin the Count of Edessa.

Baldwin was officially crowned King in the Basilica of Bethlehem on Christmas day in 1100. It was Baldwin the First who helped to establish what would become the Monastic orders. In 1112 AD he founded the "Hospitallers" whose name is the origin of the modern word "Hospital". Along with being charged with defending the citizens of the kingdom from attack, these knights were also given the special mission of caring for the sick and the injured setting up special houses to care for the ill, establishing the first hospitals.

It was Baldwin who also established the "Assizes of Jerusalem," a kind of Feudal law codex devised in order to govern and guide the new Latin population of the Crusader States. This written code was deposited in the Church of the Holy Sepulcher in Jerusalem and became known as the Letters of the Sepulcher. These letters put into written law the regulations for political office and guidelines for how civil justice should be administered. . The French Feudal based system they tried to transplant on Mid-East soil would struggle to blossom, however, and much of the old Arab system remained at the most basic level.

The main administration problem of the Crusader states would lie in the distrust and disagreement that various Counts, Dukes and Lords had for each other. The Crusaders were a diverse bunch cobbled together from various corners of the European continent united to face a common enemy, and once the main threat had subsided, some of their own differences began to fracture their hastily put together union.

These tensions would truly come to a head under the reign of the man known as the "Leper King" Baldwin the Fourth. Born in 1161 to Jerusalem's King Almaric and Queen Agnes, the young Baldwin initially seemed to be in great health. But then one day when Baldwin IV was playing with some friends his tutor made the strange observation that the child seemed to be impervious to pain. He saw the other children playing so rough with the young man, wrestling and digging their nails into him, that his arms were covered in blood.

At first everyone thought that Baldwin was just trying to show some restraint and reflect how tough he was, but after closer inspection, it was soon realized that the child didn't cry out because he really couldn't feel the wounds, his arms were completely numb; a necrosis which is the direct indication of Leprosy. This cast an immense dread and fear over those who had such high hopes for Baldwin and they worried about what kind of future he might have.

It was only three years later however, that Baldwin's father would suddenly and un-expectantly die, causing Baldwin IV to be crowned in his place. During the tumultuous period of Baldwin's succession many of the Islamic enemies of the kingdom began making aggressive moves toward Crusader state borders. And one man especially made himself rise above the others to lead the Muslim re-conquest; a man named Saladin. The real threat of Saladin actually began with a peace treaty.

Signed with the Approval of Raymond, the Regent of Tripoli (Tripoli Israel, not Libya), through a policy of appeasement, full peace was established with Saladin in 1175. The death knell to the Crusader states was the fact that the peace treaty promised to tie the Crusaders' hands when it came to the territorial gains that Saladin was making in Syria. It soon became clear, however, that this peace was simply a ruse for Saladin to build up a massive army that could encircle and destroy the Crusader states. .

Saladin had free reign to build up his arsenal, unopposed until Baldwin the Fourth, the Leper King, rose up to stop him. In 1176, just one year after the disastrous peace treaty with Saladin, a 15 year old Baldwin IV was finally given full charge of the Kingdom. Knowing that an all-out invasion by the Muslims was imminent, his first action as King was to rip to shreds the peace treaty signed with Saladin.

The Leper King then went on the offensive and sent an expeditionary force to raid the lands surrounding Damascus. This move made Saladin cease the siege he was carrying out on Aleppo and take a more defensive stance. A few months later, Baldwin IV maintained his momentum, achieving more decisive blows against Saladin in both Lebanon and Syria. Saladin's response to these incursions was swift and fierce. He sent an army of 26,000 men to lay siege to Jerusalem. It looked like certain doom to most of the denizens of Jerusalem and it was only the Leper King who still held out hope that the city could be saved.

Forcing himself up out of his sick bed, Baldwin IV, running on pure adrenalin and willpower, summoned up a small force of just 600 knights and 3000 foot soldiers and rode out to meet Saladin in battle. It was a tremendous and terrible sight to see the King who many described as "half dead" in appearance, mounted in full Zombie fashion on his steed, with only his indomitable force of will keeping him astride.

Even Saladin, knowing the horrible condition of the King and the ragtag force that he had mustered, balked at the very idea of engaging them and without batting an eye proceeded to the gates of Jerusalem. The Leper King was determined, however, and even though many of his men thought that all was lost, right before he led the charge against Saladin's massive army, Baldwin tried one more time to rally the courage of his troops.

According to testimony, the Leper King dismounted from his horse and produced the relic of the "true cross." He took this item and prostrated before it, crying out to God for success in battle. He then rose up from his prayer and urged his men to press forward. The Leper King, Baldwin IV, jumped back on his horse and led his small force directly at Saladin. Amazingly, Saladin's troops were routed and many were killed before Saladin's army went into full retreat.

It is said that Saladin barely escaped with his life. Reports also declared that spectacular supernatural phenomenon presented itself around the figure of Baldwin IV; many claimed that they saw the patron saint of soldiers, "St. George," shadowing the Leper King's every move, and others said that the True Cross Baldwin IV held in battle gave off an eerie light throughout the conflict.

But the paranormal aside, it was an amazing success for Baldwin's small expeditionary force to be able to turn back such a massive army. But this would prove to be the last major victory for the Kingdom of Jerusalem and two years later after Baldwin finally succumbs to his illness, crushing the Crusaders' wishes to establish their own Holy Estate; the Kingdom of Heaven would be no more.

CHAPTER 4

The King's Crusade

It was on Friday October 27, 1187 that Jerusalem finally found its way into the eager and capable hands of Sultan Saladin. Once this news reached Europe, it led Pope Gregory VIII to call for another Crusade; sometimes known as the "King's Crusade," this massive expedition was led by many of Europe's most important leaders including, Philip II of France, Richard the Lionheart of England, and Emperor Frederick of the Holy Roman Empire.

It was the German Frederick who initially worked as a buffer between the sometimes contentious relationship of Richard the Lionheart and France's King Philip, but his role as intermediary would not last long, since as fate would have it, Emperor Frederick would drown before ever reaching the shores of Israel, causing his own army to give up their mission. The early demise of Frederick also created an unstable relationship between the English and the French, but regardless, the two nations tried their best to march on. The Crusaders finally landed at the Port of Acre in 1191.

In total the English and French forces are said to have totaled 600,000. These men laid siege to the city of Acre and after a prolonged struggle finally managed to get the city to surrender. Meanwhile, while this was taking place, Saladin received word of the invading Crusaders and quickly summoned up an army of reinforcements, but his efforts proved to be too late and Acre was firmly in the hands of the Crusaders.

Soon after their capture of the city however, the tensions between the English and French Kings soon boiled over and in a huff of disagreement, Philip II departed back to France, living the entire crusading army in the hands of Richard the Lionheart. It was here that the British King walked onto the stage of world history and after many fierce battles, became the stuff of legend and romantic heroism. But it wasn't the exploits of Richard the Lionheart alone that were so remarkable.

Rather than heroism, it was a romance of another kind that was well documented on both sides of an apparent budding "bromance" between Richard the Lionheart and the dashing Muslim leader Saladin. Against all odds, these two who were supposed to be deadly enemies, engaged in a terrible ideological struggle, steadily grew to greatly respect each other, and not only that, by all accounts; actually liked one another.

There are several instances of kindness that the great Muslim leader showed King Richard. Such as the well documented case of sending him medicine and special fruit when he was sick. But if a get well fruit basket wasn't enough, Sultan Saladin was reported to have even given Richard an expensive Arabian Stallion when he heard that Richard's horse had been killed in battle.

Showing just how complex human relations could be, these two men who were both esteemed as kind hearted (as well as lion hearted), would soon once again find themselves fighting to the death at the gates of Jerusalem. Richard, however, was never able to take the city and all of his fighting ended in a truce with Saladin, in which the Muslim leader agreed to end extracting taxes from Christian pilgrims visiting Jerusalem while it remained under Islamic control.

Saladin also agreed to recognize the Christian settlements along the coast from Jaffa to Tyre, promising to leave them undisturbed as well. This first sort of Mid-East peace agreement was really a major breakthrough in diplomatic relations, but back home in Europe, where people expected nothing short of absolute surrender of the Holy Land, most regarded this negotiation as a bitter failure. Richard the Lionheart then departed shortly after this truce, but after a series of bad luck managed to get shipwrecked off the coast of the Adriatic.

He then attempted to disguise himself as he traveled through Austria, since he knew that the Duke of Austria desired his capture due to some previous disagreements at the outset of the Crusade. And so it was that the man who was supposed to be the great Crusading hero of Europe had to sneak back into his homeland like a fugitive.

The Duke's forces soon found Richard and put him in chains. The King was then only able to buy his freedom by paying out a huge sum of money which was said to be double the annual revenues of the entire state of England; thus bringing a very unceremonious end to the King's Crusade.

CHAPTER 5

The Self Defeating Crusade

The Fourth Crusade launched by Pope Innocent III in 1202 was issued as a desperate attempt to retake so many of the lost gains of the previous Crusades. As evidenced in the dramatic speech Innocent III gave to his audience, "How does a man love according to divine precept his neighbor as himself when, knowing that his Christian brothers in faith and in name are held by the perfidious Muslims in strict confinement and weighed down by the yoke of heaviest servitude, he does not devote himself to the task of freeing them? Is it by chance that you do not know that many thousands of Christians are bound in slavery and imprisoned by the Muslims, tortured with innumerable torments?"

This time there was a change of plans, however, and since so many repeated assaults through the north of Israel had failed, a new strategy was devised that would allow the Crusaders to attack through Egypt. Military strategists had been leaning towards an advance on Egypt for a while since they knew that a major power base of the region was there. They also knew that if they could topple Egypt, they could march through the Sinai directly to Jerusalem, virtually unopposed. In order to do this, however, they would need a fleet of ships to launch the assault.

It was decided that they would partner with the huge merchant community of Venice in order to acquire the appropriate ships and material to launch their offensive. The Venetians, due to trading concessions made by the Byzantine Empire in exchange for military service in the years previous, had become the wealthiest merchants in Constantinople, as a consequence they drove nearly all of the local merchants out of business.

This had created a very tense situation of resentment towards them and these tensions had boiled over in 1182 when a large chunk of the 60,000 Venetians living in Constantinople were massacred by the city's angry local population. It was in the backdrop of this conflict that the Crusaders had arrived at Constantinople and as the city was on the brink of civil war, their financial sponsors, the Venetians, demanded that they choose a side. Feeling they had no choice but to side with their financial backers, and in a twist of irony, the Crusaders who from the very beginning had been called to protect the Byzantines wound up sacking their city.

But there was quite a level political manipulation on the part of the Venetians that led the Crusaders to this treacherous act. The Venetians, who had their own axe to grind, convinced the Crusaders that the current leader of the Byzantine Empire was a corrupt, power hungry threat who had allowed the massacres of Westerners in his kingdom. The Venetians then produced a supposed royal; political exile, Byzantine Prince Alexius Angelus, who claimed that his father, Emperor Isaac II was the rightful leader of Byzantium.

The Prince then told them that if they agreed to free his father he would pay them 200,000 silver marks, which would be more than enough to pay off their debt to the Venetians and also further finance their expedition to the Holy Land. It was through this political intrigue and the promise of a reward that the plan was hatched for the Crusaders to depose the current Byzantine emperor and install the imprisoned former leader onto the throne in his place.

This was a major part of the plot engineered by the Venetians since they knew that the Crusaders were going broke paying for their ship building services. It was through this ploy that the Crusaders immediately fell into the trap of Venetian and Byzantine politics. The Crusaders would be surprised once again however after their installation of Isaac II when this new Byzantine ruler revealed that he was absolutely broke.

Feeling double-crossed, the angry Crusaders could not hold back their fury any longer and decided to get what they could not achieve through diplomacy by force and laid siege to the city carrying off vast amounts of wealth, it was these stolen riches that the Crusaders used to pay the Venetians for the fleet.

Pope Innocent III strongly denounced these actions but being far away in Rome there was not much more he could personally do about it. Unfortunately for the Byzantines they would never quite recover from this blow and it was this deliberate assault by their previously sworn protectors that weakened the Byzantine Empire just enough to allow it to completely collapse in the face of the Turks in 1452, very much defeating the original call to the Crusade in the first place.

CHAPTER 6

The Final Crusades

The last few Crusades to be launched barely gained any headway at all. There was the fifth Crusade that repeated the attempt of the fourth to seize Egypt, whose only success was the seizing of the town of Damietta in 1219. The Crusaders then launched an ill-fated attack on Cairo and were decisively repelled, the Crusaders and the Egyptian Sultan then agreed on an eight year peace agreement.

And so it was, barely 8 years later in 1228 that Emperor Frederick II launched what is known as the Sixth Crusade. . But amazingly, when his forces landed in Jerusalem very little fighting actually occurred and what no one could achieve with force Frederick managed to achieve with diplomacy. After several rounds of talks he actually convinced the Sultan to hand over Jerusalem, Nazareth, and Bethlehem to the Crusaders for a ten year period. The agreement gave the Christians complete control with the one exception that the Al Aksa mosque and the Dome of the Rock maintain their Muslim authority, a move that was incredibly unpopular to his own fellow Muslims.

The Seventh Crusade was then brought on when the Muslims who were disaffected by the previous agreement stormed the city in 1244. The Crusaders attempted to respond but were so outnumbered that their army was completely defeated within 48 hours. King Louis IX of France then rose up as the leader of the new Crusade and on August 25, 1248, he amassed a force of about 35,000 men and sent a fleet to Egypt. The King seemingly was taking his time, however, and instead of going to Egypt right away, he ended up spending the whole winter in Cyprus. His expeditionary force didn't end up landing in Egypt until the following year in June of 1249.

The King's enthusiasm hadn't waned any though, and as excited as ever, he was the first to jump on land and plant the flag of St. Denis on the outskirts of the Egyptian port city of Damietta. After a brief resistance his men were able to take over the town. The army then trudged on from there all the way to Cairo where the rain-swollen waters of the Nile began to slow down their progress.

It was in this water-logged fashion that they finally reached the citadel of Al Mansurah and attempted to lay siege to it. After several failures, the group finally decided to build a pontoon bridge in order to break the defenses of the Citadel. The battle was long and fierce and resulted in the death of the King's brother Robert of Artois. After a prolonged struggle the Crusaders finally seemed to be gaining the upper hand but the army was completely exhausted and sickness broke out among most of the soldiers.

Demoralized, King Louis had to order his men to retreat back to Damietta. It was an utter humiliation and embarrassment for King Louis and he and his men were incessantly harassed by the pursuing Egyptian army. Their pursuers managed to capture them before they ever reached Damietta and the King was held prisoner until his benefactors could pay out a large amount of money to the Egyptians to secure his release.

Upon gaining his freedom, King Louis IX left for Acre where he managed to succeed diplomatically where he had failed militarily and brokered several peace deals to secure the safety of many Christian cities in Syria. These diplomatic successes were not enough to lessen the King's crusading spirit however, and in 1270 he embarked on what is known as the Eighth Crusade which had him again leading an army, this time to come to the aid of the last Crusader states in Syria.

But for some reason, his men never made it to Syria and instead were diverted to Tunis where, after leading battles for two months, Louis IX passed away and his Crusading ambition left with him. One final attempt at a Crusade was then issued a year later by King Edward of England but accomplished very little and the King and his men left Syria after achieving a weak sort of truce with its Islamic leaders, making his attempt the Ninth and final Crusade.

In the following years, the Crusader states would all disappear. In 1268 Antioch was overrun, in 1289 Tripoli was wiped out, and in 1291 that last Christian stronghold of Acre was no more. The remaining Christians of these doomed cities were given the choices of fleeing, being massacred, or being enslaved with no hope of a final, last minute Crusade on the horizon to save them.

CHAPTER 7

The Post-Crusade World

After the last call for a Crusade had drawn to a close, the Muslim Turkish Empire had mostly free rein and was quickly closing in on their old rivals, , the Byzantine Empire. And by 1400 the Byzantines had been reduced to little more than the city-state of Constantinople. Knowing the end was coming soon, the Emperor began to travel all over Europe in an effort to raise awareness of their plight and in hopes of encouraging another Crusade on their behalf.

He went to Denmark, Germany and even as far as England requesting aid, but his pleas were mostly met with deaf ears. Europe was tired of Crusading, it seemed, and could no longer be convinced to send enormous manpower and money to aid the declining Christians of the east. And when it came to the Pope of Rome, the Emperor could only get his ear if he pledged to deny the Orthodox faith and convert his kingdom to Catholicism, something the people of Constantinople would never agree to.

So it was that the Empire's age old foes, the Turks, found their enemy completely alone and isolated and to further ensure that they stayed that way in 1451, Turkish Sultan Mehmet II positioned his men and took complete control of the Bosphorus Strait, closing access to the Black Sea and blocking the Byzantines from even leaving Constantinople. The Turks were hoping to block any possible reinforcements from coming to the Byzantines' aid.

This effort was mostly successful but 700 elite Italian soldiers under the command of Giovanni Giustiniani did manage to break through and worked with the Byzantines to help them to reinforce the walls of the city. Byzantine Emperor Constantine did his best to make sure that the massive Theodosian walls were repaired and that the walls in the northern Blachnae district were also strengthened. To prevent a naval attack he also shut off the harbors placing giant chains across them so no ship could enter.

The main force of the Ottoman army arrived just outside of Constantinople on April 1, ' 1453 and began preparing their staging area the next day. The centerpiece of the Ottoman siege equipment was a giant cannon that they used to batter the Theodosian walls. This canon was the pride and joy of the Ottoman army but it wasn't enough to break down the Byzantine defenses. And after creating very little damage, the cannon took three hours to reload, giving the Byzantines ample time to repair any damage that may have occurred. The uselessness of the cannon was then followed by the embarrassment of the Ottoman fleet being unable to penetrate the chained up harbors.

And in their chaos they allowed four Christian ships to break through them on April 20. The Turkish leader Mehmet then ordered for the fleet to be pushed forward over greased logs so they could be pushed over and refloated behind the chain. Constantine then quickly directed more of his men to stand guard at the Golden Horn walls to defend against a possible breach.

Meanwhile, after repeatedly attacking the Theodosian walls without much result, apparently thinking if he couldn't break through, he would go underneath them, Mehmet had his soldiers start to dig tunnels under the walls, but these efforts were defeated at every turn. Extremely frustrated, Mehmet called a meeting with his commanders and determined that a final all-out assault would be issued on May 28. ,

After intense struggle, his army finally managed to break through the Byzantine defenses and started to pour through the city. Constantine was believed to have died in battle shortly after this and Constantinople soon suffered through massive massacres and plundering at the hands of the Turks. The fall of Constantinople was felt all over the Christian world and the Pope immediately called for another crusade in order to recover the lost city, but still no one would answer the call, and it appeared that with the end of Constantinople, so came the end of the Crusades.

This would mark a period of drastic change for Europe, with the arrival of Greek refugees, and an influx of previously unknown information about medicine and the arts would usher in the Renaissance. The loss of Constantinople, denying Europe access to the east, would also launch the age of exploration and many have noted that if it wasn't for the fall of Constantinople there may not have been such a push for a Christopher Columbus to discover the Americas.

It was just a few decades after the loss of Constantinople in 1492 that Columbus was sanctioned to discover an easier route to Asia, and since all land access was cut off, of course this meant a voyage over the sea. But very few people realize that along with finding a safe passage to Asia for the Spanish government, Christopher Columbus had an ulterior motive of his own. A deeply religious man, he sought to recover enough wealth and riches from his travels in order to finance another Crusade!

Christopher Columbus the Crusader may sound a bit far-fetched for some, but it is not. It is a well-documented fact that Christopher Columbus was seeking to finance another Crusade. Christopher Columbus repeated this intent in written documents all throughout his life. Even his last will and testament stated that he wanted nothing more than for his estate to finance the launch of another Crusade to the Holy Land.

In fact there are more than ninety documents that bear testament to this desire. He was trying his best to get the world interested in another rescue mission of the Christian lands in the East. But sadly enough for Mr. Columbus, for all of his efforts, he was led back to Europe in chains, in debt to the Spanish government. And since the European powers didn't realize exactly what it was that Columbus had discovered until decades after his death. He died a broken man, feeling like he was a failure in his mission, unable to amass the resources necessary for another Crusade.

Meanwhile the Christian world was increasingly on the defensive and the Muslim armies were on the march, leading right up to the Battle of Lepanto. Lepanto is a little known island in the Gulf of Patras. And although the location remains obscure, the resulting battles that this piece of real estate inspired are not. Lepanto was controlled by the Venetians until the Ottomans had captured it in 1499 and transformed it into one of their eleven districts in the Province of Cezayir. This was yet another frightening loss for the Europeans.

Just decades after the loss of Constantinople in the east, the Ottomans were now knocking on their door in the west, with this island giving them dominance over the Mediterranean and a clear launching pad for an invasion of Italy. This was a very real threat and it wouldn't be long before the Pope would be calling for something very similar to the old clarion call for a Crusade in order to put it down.

No one may have said the word "Crusade" but when Pope Pius V organized what he called the "Holy League" consisting of; "The Papacy, Spain, Parma, Malta, Savoy, Genoa, Ferraa, and the Princes of Tuscany, it was the old Crusading ideals that came to the forefront. Even the inclusion of Malta was a direct testament to this because the Island of Malta was the very last holdout of what could be considered a Crusader state.

This so called "Holy League" then set sail toward the Gulf of Patrikos near Lepanto and were given orders to engage the Turks in battle on October 7, 1571. The Christian force was said to have consisted of 6 large Venetian ships, 207 oar propelled galleys carrying 30,000 soldiers and some additional auxiliary vehicles. The Turkish force was much larger but not quite as well equipped.

The most alarming feature of the Turkish force was the sheer number of soldiers that it boasted. With expeditionary regiments that easily held about 100,000 men, they clearly outnumbered the Holy League. In fact, when the Christian ships were less than 15 miles from the Turkish fleet, the breadth of the Turkish armada was a stunning sight and appeared to stretch from shore to shore of the Gulf.

But the Holy League pushed on and soon the flagships of both fleets began engaging each other. The Holy League then regrouped and sent its six heavily armed Venetian ships a mile in advance of the Christian frontline. As it turns out this was the first time that high walled Galleasses were used in battle and the Turks didn't know what to make of it; having never seen these kinds of ships before, they actually mistook them to be Merchant ships.

Thinking that the Merchant ships had made a miscalculation or were somehow in distress, the Turkish ships pursued them, thinking that they would be an easy mark that they could loot and retrieve cargo from. But when the Galleasses turned around and lowered their guns down on the Turks; they would have been in for the shock of their lives. The Venetian ships unloaded on the Turkish fleet that had come to intercept them and in the process managed to sink 70 Turkish galleys before the real battle had even begun. Their fortune then started to take another turn for the worse as the winds literally shifted in the favor of the Holy League.

The Holy Leaguers quickly took advantage of the headwind and lifted their sails to charge the Turkish fleet that was becoming dead in the water. The Muslim flagship "Sultana" then hurled itself at the Christian flagship in a ramming attack that locked both ships into a life and death struggle, turning the decks of the vessels into one single battlefield. The tide began to turn against the Muslims however, when after hours of intense fighting the captain of the ship, Ali Pasha was killed and the Sultana was taken over by the Christians.

The battle was all but over at this point and at the end of the day the Turkish fleet was almost completely annihilated along with 117 galleys that the Christians managed to capture. The Holy League also managed to free 15,000 enslaved Christians, all of whom who had presumably been kidnapped or made prisoner from previous wars. The unofficial Crusaders of the Holy League managed to deal a demoralizing blow to the Turkish advance.

The Holy League proved to be invaluable in its success against the Ottoman Turks during this major sea battle, but it was a land battle that would bring in an even more spectacular Holy League victory at the gates of Vienna. Known as the Battle of Vienna, the Turkish threat began in earnest when an army of some 90,000 Turkish soldiers amassed on the outskirts of Vienna in 1683 and through an official messenger, sent to the city the ultimatum, "Accept Islam and live in peace under the Sultan!"

The people of Vienna adamantly refused this "request" and the assault on the city began a few hours later. In just a matter of days the Turks managed to completely surround the city. Despite having to beat back constant attacks, the city's defenders successfully held them back. Then, trying a tactic that had been used in Constantinople some 200 years before, the Turks began digging tunnels under the city walls so they could place explosives at strategic points, hoping to cause sections of the fortification to collapse.

The Austrians fought back, however, and dug their own tunnels where they placed explosives of their own to disrupt the Turkish army. The constant bombardment would take its toll, however, and soon the city walls were little more than rubble and the Christian defenders had been whittled down to little more than about 4000 fighting men. Vienna seemed to be on its last leg, ready to collapse at any time, but unknown to the Turks, a new Crusade was on its way in the form of another Holy League consisting of 60,000 men from a multitude of different European states headed by King John III Sobieski of Poland.

This group marched through the mountainous forest of the Wienerwald and approached Vienna from the west. The Ottomans never imagined that anyone would be able to bring an army through the no man's land of the Wienerwald forests and as a result, had left this ring of their defense largely undefended. The Turkish authority would be greatly dismayed, however, when the combined strength of this Christian Army emerged through the trees on Saturday September 11, 1683, a day that would go down in infamy for the Turkish forces.

Kara Mustafa, the leading authority of the attack, was informed of the incursion they faced in their rear flank and was advised to momentarily call off the siege so they could regroup against the new threat. Mustafa, however, was so completely obsessed with taking the city that he refused to listen and instead intensified his siege of Vienna and only allowed a small force of a few thousand infantry, a few thousand cavalry and a few cannons, to go fight the Holy League that was Crusading right at his back.

The united front of the Holy League pushed this interception force to the side and was soon tearing right through the main army of the Ottoman Turks. It is said that by 4 pm, the Holy League had the victory, taking down the Turkish force on all sides. And as day started to turn into night the decisively routed Turks had no choice but to give up on the assault and flee back into the Balkans. The battle was over and Vienna was saved, all thanks to a bunch of Crusaders known as the Holy League.

The Islamic force of the Ottoman Turks had terrified European Christians for centuries and the Battle of Vienna was the culmination of that terror, stabbing at the heart of Europe, and no matter how some would like to sugar coat it, the fact remains that these Islamic extremists posed a very real threat to Christian Europe's very existence. Through their will and determination, the Crusades and Holy Leagues were dispatched to take on this threat, not by choice but out of necessity, in order to defend their very existence from annihilation.

Fortunately for the free world of today these men were successful in beating this belligerent force back and after the Battle of Vienna, the Ottoman Empire began a long decline into the dust bin of history, soon becoming the "sick man of Europe" and no longer a threat to anyone.

And as much as a tainted popular opinion loves to hold these men in contempt; the men who fought so bravely in the Crusades should not have to apologize for making the world a safer place. They were not marauding monsters just looking for a fight like the modern revisionists and the ill-informed would like to believe, these men were nothing short of the last line of defense for Western Civilization. And for those of us who enjoy the ideals of Western democracy and liberty, in the end, we owe it all to the peace that was established in the Post Crusader world.

Printed by Amazon Italia Logistica S.r.l.
Torrazza Piemonte (TO), Italy